A New Thought on Blue

A New Thought on Blue:

An Anthology of Ocean Poems by Third Grade Poets

Edited by Erica Krug

Dedication and Acknowledgments

We dedicate this book to Sylvia Earle for inspiring us and to all of the sea creatures in the ocean.

We also dedicate it to our families, friends and pets.

We thank Dan Walkner's East High Mass Media Class, Gillian Nevers and the Wisconsin Fellowship of Poets, Shannon and Dave Furman, Sebastian Vang, Peggy Moore, the inspiration of the Greater Madison Writing Project and all of the people who donated money and time to this project. Without you, it wouldn't have been possible.

Never doubt that a small group of thoughtful committed citizens can change the world; indeed, it's the only thing that ever has.
-Margaret Mead

With every drop of water you drink, every breath you take, you're connected to the sea. No matter where on Earth you live.
-Sylvia Earle

Introduction

We might not live by the ocean, but we are a part of it. From puddles to ponds, ponds to streams, streams to rivers, rivers to lakes, lakes to the ocean; everything is connected. We can't last a day without the ocean.

We are third graders from Lake View Elementary School and we care. We first learned about the ocean this year when we read a book about oceanographer Sylvia Earle. We learned that the ocean needs protection. We also learned about Earle's organization called Mission Blue, which is working to protect areas of the ocean called "hope spots." We decided to write a book of poems to help raise money for Mission Blue. We named our book "A New Thought on Blue" because we want our poems to help people think about the ocean in a different way.

We hope you enjoy our poems and original linoleum cut prints.

Eliana, Luke, Margot, Suchart and Erica Krug

Madison, Wisconsin
May 2013

All proceeds from this book will be donated to Mission Blue. For more information, please visit: http://www.thesealliance.org/

How to be a Sea Dragon

Jack, age 9

Be gone

Touch sea stars

Look more like some body

Go slow

Be red, yellow, green and brown

Keep going and do not stop

Be tall and straight

Be brave

The Walrus
Margot, age 9 1/2

Big and fat
Like a blubber balloon on land.
Battling the polar bear,
But ruler of the sea.
Some win, some lose.
Pulling itself onto land
With sword-like tusks.
Pushing the bear into the sea,
Down he goes.
Down, down to the sea.
When hungry,
Goes down to eat clams
Dusting sand off, like a maid.
The storms come
Going up with their built-in floatie,
But some ice freezes
No way out.
The walrus has one more trick
Up his flipper.
Bashing the ice with his head
Like a brick,
The walrus is ruler
Of the sea.

Clown Fish

Vai, age 8

Clownfish
Orange white
Swim hide clean
Sea anemone coral reef shark whale sunlight zone
Wave crash sparkle
Still blue
Ocean

How to be a Sea Lion

Lindsay, age 8

Swim in the sea
Be silky and smooth
Go, "Art, art, art, art."
Catch your fish
When you're five months old
Eat five to ten pounds a day
Live in rookeries
Spend lots of time
In the ocean.

Sea Turtle

Luis, age 9 ½

In the coral reef
nothing is as beautiful
as green hard-shelled Loggerhead Sea Turtle.
In November, crabs beware because the
loggerheads are getting closer and closer and...
SNAP!

Emperor Penguins

Suchart, age 9

The penguins are in Antarctica

There are baby penguins hatching

The penguins are huddling up to keep warm

Baby penguins are going back to their dads'
blubber

Emperor penguins are on an iceberg traveling to a
new ice land

Penguins are going into the water to feed their
baby penguins

Beluga

Robert, age 9

At the bottom of the sea
with
no
light
except angler fish.
Beluga's skin
shimmers in darkness.
Friends of almost every creature in the sea.
Fish, dolphins, sharks, seals.
Traveling north to south,
south to north.
Showing off how beautiful
it really is.

Sea Horse

Eliana, age 9

Mysteriously clings onto seaweed
Colorfully and cheerfully sways side to side
On seaweed vines.
Act fierce and strong
Camouflage to stay safe
Hunt in the clear sand for supper
Curl yourself up and uncurl yourself
Be a sea horse.

Moray Eel

Hayden, age 8

Glinting teeth
In a cave beneath.
It's a moray eel!
And it wants a meal
From your hand.
Plastic bags it wants to ban.

Orcas

Luke, age 8

Orcas jumping

Orcas eating

Orcas swimming

Orcas hunting

Orcas spy-hopping

Orcas diving

Orcas making big waves

Orcas being playful

Orcas making clicks and whistles.

Dolphin

Kayla, age 8

Dolphins laughing

Baby dolphin watched mother

Mother dolphin goes up for a minute to watch the
sunset go down

Sea Otter

Elyse, age 8 ¾

Frolicking in the grassy sea meadows
Where they are not prey
They are playing amongst their friends and never
seem to be alone
And silly little faces peeking through the grasses
and then just seeping away from you
But they always come back, but
Beware- they can always talk behind your back!
They're not afraid of each other, only predators
And maybe you too sometimes
But the rest they are just tiny little creatures
Frolicking in the icy green blue waters
Upon the mist and coldness though
They are just like you- need a place to like and live
and have to have some friends and a thing to eat
Do not judge them by their cuteness even if
they're so
Say to yourself 'they're a mammal just like you'
But they live under water and have furry friends
In a play set made of coral
And a house made out of sticks
I can't believe I'm saying this
But we're just like them in a way
Believe it

Shark

Paxton, age 9

Shark
Sharp smooth
Snaking sneaking smashes
Shrimp slits seals squid
Stalking slamming splashing
Sleek silent
Swimmer

Whale

Jordan, age 9

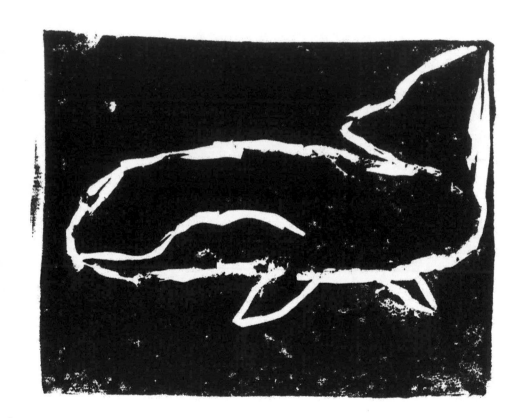

Whales

Gray and white

They splash

They eat

They sing

Whales communicate

They eat fish and seaweed and look for prey

Sharks are their enemies

Lobster Haiku

They look like big crabs
Conga line through the ocean
They have big sharp claws

Squid Haiku

Bright colors all around
Squid are marine animals
Some squid are giants

Hayden, age 8

Cuttlefish

Three-hearted, green-blue blooded creature
Are you glad you don't have those for a feature?
How do they eat?
Well, that is kind of neat
The tongue inches out
Then, "SNAP"
That fish got lucky
But next time it could get a little yucky
I'd say, they're the alien of the sea
But could this fish be cuddly?
Someone might figure out this mystery
But, one thing's for sure
It's not going to be me.

Lindsay, age 8

How to be a Penguin

Huddle and take turns in the middle
Go swimming and eat fish
Share your food with your little brother or sister
Wear a tuxedo and a white shirt
Hold your eggs between your legs

Luis, age 9 1/2

How to be a Sting Ray

Flap your wings

Be sneaky

Swing your tail

Mate once a year

Have two to six babies

Have babies inside you

Eat clams and other invertebrates

Have many relatives

Be flat and long

Lie on the sandy floor

Live in the ocean

Be camouflaged

Elyse, age 8 ¾

How to be a Plastic Bag

Pollute the ocean
Invade the species of sea turtles and sea lions
Fly around town
Making the air dirty
Get banned in San Francisco,
Africa, China, and Seattle
Stop being used!
Be a plastic bag.

Eliana, age 9

Extinction

Pollution killing,
Plastic bags destroying,
Extinction will come.
We can't do it alone.
We need help.

Margot, age 9 1/2

How to be a Fish

Swim away from sharks
Hide in plants
Swim fast
Stay under water for a long time
Swim
Eat small fish and plants
Make lots of bubbles
Swim deep into the ocean
Do not drown
Be playful.

Luke, age 8

Sea Otter

Lying on its back
Eating California stars
Holding hands
Turning circles
Singing songs
Having the most fun of your life
Splashing water on your head
Teeth turning lavender
You are not alone
Eighty pounds
Scrunchy nose

Robert, age 9

How to be a Dolphin

Ocean ocean ocean

A baby dolphin is swimming in the ocean

He sees different creatures

He sees a sea otter holding paws with his friend

He is going to see other creatures

He is going on an adventure

Suchart, age 9

The Ocean

Move frantically and calmly
Be the heart of the world
Make big waves
Be the home to all sea creatures
Make oxygen for the people of this world
Be important
Be our ocean.

Eliana, age 9

Three Diamante Poems

Dolphin
Gray playful
Swim flips jumps
Sea star sea shell sting ray sea lion
Diving hunting eating
Crunchy smooth
Shark

Beluga
Large enormous
Swimming eating diving
Humpback cat cheese icicles
Scamper run walk
Brown skinny
Mouse

Octopus
Sticky inky
Squirt throw beak
Break cave arms water
Wiggle tuttle swim
Polka-dotty smooth
Squid

Collaborative class poems with Gillian and James
from the Wisconsin Fellowship of Poets

Sea Turtle Song

Sea turtle, sea turtle swimming in the sea
Look at the plastic bag driftin' toward me
Don't eat it sea turtle, leave it be
Help sea turtle and me
So ban plastic bags with me

Sea turtle, sea turtle swimming in the sea
Look at the plastic bag driftin' toward me
Don't eat it sea turtle, leave it be
Help sea turtle and me
So ban plastic bags with me

Margot, age 9 ½

Indigo Daydreams

Erica Krug

Indigo daydreams
Unravel the moon
Cast a shimmering line
to the midnight surface

Cobalt salt
Driftwood stars
Navy beasts
Green sea glass jars

Slate gray whirlpools with swirling kelp
High tides ebb while low tides rise
and castles melt away
Sway sea dragon, sway

Buoy whales in your waves
Rock otters to sleep
Hum tranquil mermaid songs through the
salty deep

Visions of Neptune

Dan Walkner

I've never seen the ocean
But I've had a vision of Neptune
Head in his hands, pondering his kingdom.
Thieves, intruders and vandals
False beliefs, polluters and scandals
As the Natives passed a peace pipe to their future
conquerors,
He calmed the seas while the naïve pin prick of
opportunity became the twisting knife of progress.
Neptune stands and thrusts his triton high.
Tides rise and torrents empty the sky
Jetties swirl and hurricanes rage.
The third act begins as the actors take the stage
The final curtain washes upon a pebbled beach.
Silence reigns upon the lands
A tired, victorious Neptune is free to wash his
hands.

Made in the USA
Lexington, KY
19 July 2013